# GLOUCESTER
## THEN & NOW
### IN COLOUR

DARREL KIRBY

WITH ADDITIONAL PHOTOGRAPHY BY KEN JACQUES

*This book is dedicated to my wife Sharon and my mum, who are both very proud to see my books in print. And to my dad, who would also have been proud – and not a little surprised.*

First published in 2012

The History Press
The Mill, Brimscombe Port
Stroud, Gloucestershire, GL5 2QG
www.thehistorypress.co.uk

British Library Cataloguing in Publication Data.
A catalogue record for this book is available from the British Library.

ISBN 978 0 7524 6476 3

Typesetting and origination by The History Press
Printed in Turkey.

# CONTENTS

# ACKNOWLEDGEMENTS

I extend a huge thank you to everyone who has helped me in putting together this book and/or have had to put up with me while I've been working on it. In particular my thanks go to Ken Jacques for helping with the photography, his tutorials in the use of Photoshop and his general enthusiasm for the project. It's nice to find someone that is even more of an anorak about taking pictures of the city than I am!

As always the staff at the Gloucestershire Archives were extremely helpful, making life for me as easy as possible in trawling through the huge number of photographs in their care and providing guidance on the thorny issue of copyright.

Thanks also to everyone who provided photographs for use in this book. Finding suitable 'Then' photographs was not always easy. I have tried my best to identify and contact everyone whose photographs I have used, but if I have used any without permission I apologise profusely.

Finally, as always, my biggest thanks go to my wife Sharon, without whose support and tolerance this book wouldn't have been possible.

# PICTURE CREDITS

Unless otherwise stated, the pictures in this book were either taken by me or come from my own collection of postcards with no obvious point of contact for copyright. The other pictures are produced with the kind permission of the following:

Reproduced from a Frith & Co postcard: p. 6–7, 26–7
Gloucestershire Archives: p. 31, 44–5, 52, 62–3, 66–7, 70–1, 72–3, 76–7, 80–1, 91, 93
Taken by Gwladys Davies: p. 18–19, 42
Taken by Sidney Pitcher: p. 12–13, 14–15, 17, 24–5, 36–37, 60–1, 82–3, 95
Gloucestershire Media: p. 32–3, 74–5
Ken Jacques: p. 13, 19, 20, 55, 65, 67, 68–9, 71, 78, 83, 85, 92
Reflections of Clapham Group/Bernard Polson: p. 20–1
Geoff Sandles: p. 8–9, 10–11
Reg Woolford: p. 54–5

# INTRODUCTION

Much has changed in Gloucester since the earliest photographic records, which exist from around the mid-nineteenth century. At that time Gloucester was being reshaped by the industrial revolution, fuelled by the arrival of the canal and the railways. Since then change has pretty much been a constant.

The industrial revolution led to workers flooding into the city, all of whom had to be housed. Much of this housing became slums and was swept away during the twentieth century in huge redevelopments. Punctuated by two world wars, this work culminated in the Jellicoe plan of the 1960s and '70s. Most of us look back in horror on the destruction wrought during that period, when many fine old buildings were demolished to make way for large, ugly, brutalist structures, including a number of multi-storey car parks, the unlovely Eastgate Shopping Centre and King's Square.

This was followed by a sad period of neglect for the city, but the decline is now being reversed with a host of new developments taking place or planned for the near future. Initial development of the docks started in the 1980s, but really took off from 2001 and was followed by the Quays development, which has transformed a derelict industrial wasteland into retail and leisure use.

Further developments are planned for the centre of the city. Work has now commenced on Greyfriars; the redevelopment of King's Square and the bus station also seems close to being finally realised and there are further plans for the future. This has not been without controversy, but generally the outlook for Gloucester seems to be more optimistic than it has been for a long time.

This makes it an excellent time to try to capture the changes that have taken place in the city. In carrying out this project it became very clear just how much things had changed: in places it is difficult to even identify where the old pictures were taken as nothing now remains. On the other hand, it is surprising how often very little seems to have changed: the buildings may be put to different uses, but they still survive and are generally under-appreciated. Perhaps we only appreciate our great architecture once it is too late.

# NORTHGATE STREET

THIS IS THE view down Northgate Street from the Cross. The biggest change since the older photograph was taken in 1949 is the pedestrianisation, introduced in 1992. Although controversial, it was a great change for the better in my opinion. The older photograph shows how crowded it was squeezing between shoppers and the safety barriers around the Cross. I can distinctly remember being squeezed in there waiting for the traffic lights to change, allowing you to cross the busy, traffic-clogged road.

How much better it is now to be able to wander along the spacious traffic-free streets. Otherwise, not much has changed, just the building in the foreground on the right of the picture and the fashions. Clearly the merchandise has changed, however, with three of the nearest four shops now selling mobile phones. Beyond that, in the older photograph is Stead & Simpson's shoe shop. This was there until relatively recently, but in the modern picture the store is empty. Next to that there is little change to the New Inn, then we have the impressive 1930s buildings built as part of the Oxebode Development including, hiding behind a tree in the modern picture, Debenhams, formerly the Bon Marché.

*(Author's Collection / Darrel Kirby)*

# LONDON ROAD

THESE PICTURES SHOW London Road, looking up the hill towards Wotton Pitch. When the older picture was taken in 1882, horses still provided the main means of transport. These horse-drawn trams operated in the city from 1879, but were replaced by electric trams in 1904. The glasshouse on the left was part of Paradise Nursery, but is now gone. The other Victorian buildings beyond that do still exist, but they are hidden by bushes in the modern picture.

The building on the right was the New Inn; this was a beer house by 1872 and changed its name to England's Glory in about 1984. It was one of three pubs all within a few yards of each other, the others being the York House, which is also still trading, and the Denmark Arms which closed in about 1919. In the distance are the two twelfth-century leper hospitals: St Mary Magdalene's Chapel on the left, in Hillfield Gardens, and St Margaret's Chapel on the opposite side of the road. Hillfield Gardens are also home to the King's Board and Scriven's Conduit, both originally sited in the centre of the city, but removed in the eighteenth century.

*(Geoff Sandles / Darrel Kirby)*

# KINGSHOLM ROAD

KINGSHOLM WAS THE site of the original Roman fort in
Gloucester in the late AD 40s, before the Romans moved to
what is now the centre of Gloucester in about
AD 68. The Saxons later built a great timber hall here, which
acted as a major seat of government, along with Winchester
and Westminster, until the twelfth century. The Domesday
Book may have been ordered from this great hall. By the time
the older picture was taken in about 1907, the hamlet of
Kingsholm had expanded with the building of houses in the
1850s – particularly working-class houses in the area that
became known as Clapham, in the roads behind these more
substantial Victorian properties.

The area was also home to Gloucester Rugby Club, who moved here in 1891, but it is on the opposite side of the road so can't be seen in these pictures. The Kingsholm Inn is recognisable in both pictures: this was here by at least 1847. The electric tram in the older picture is of the type that in 1904 replaced the horse-drawn trams seen on page 8. They were in turn replaced by buses in 1929.

*(Geoff Sandles / Darrel Kirby)*

# ST ALDATE STREET & KING STREET

I LOVE THIS old picture taken by Sidney Pitcher in the 1920s: things have changed so much that it took me a while to work out where it was taken from. The road going off to the left, closed off by a barrier in this picture, was King Street, now King's Walk. To the right is St Aldate Street, where you can see St Aldate's Restaurant and, next door, the Milkmaid Inn. The buildings are all closed and boarded up, awaiting demolition for the creation of King's Square (see pp. 38–9). Until recently the area where these buildings stood was the site of a 1970s monstrosity known as 'the bear pit', a large brick structure leading down to public toilets and a long-closed underpass.

The building work that can be seen in the modern picture, taken in September 2011, is the demolition of 'the bear pit', which has now been levelled to make the area more usable until a full revamp of the area takes place as part of the King's Quarter regeneration. The building on the far right of the older picture was known as St Aldate Chambers and was home to J. Pearce Pope & Sons, auctioneers. This was replaced by the modern building, now Chambers pub, in the 1980s.

*(Gloucestershire Archives / Ken Jacques)*

13

# BERKELEY STREET

THIS IS BERKELEY STREET looking toward Westgate Street. It is quite difficult to reconcile the two pictures, but a point of reference remains on the right, where a sign for the Fountain Inn can be seen. The building that it is attached to has since been demolished, enlarging the Fountain's courtyard. Buildings on the right beyond the Fountain remain, but those in the foreground were demolished to make way for the Telephone Exchange, which is set further back and therefore cannot be seen in the modern picture. At the far end of the road on the left was the Gresham Hotel which, along with the other buildings on that side of the street, was demolished in about 1910 to make way for the extension to the Shire Hall, which dominates the modern picture. At the same time the road was widened, revealing a glimpse of the cathedral at the end of the street. The modern picture is taken from slightly further back, and the building in the foreground on the left survives from that period – it is the end of a terrace of three town houses dating from about 1770, all of which have now been converted into flats.

*(Gloucestershire Archives / Darrel Kirby)*

15

# ST JOHN'S LANE

THE OLDER PICTURE here shows St John's Lane in 1920. The bridge over the lane bears the words 'The Citizen & Gloucester Journal'. The *Citizen* newspaper was started by Samuel Bland in 1876 and was originally located in St John's Hall on the right-hand side of the lane. Opposite was an old beer house with brewhouse, which Bland bought, linking the two buildings with the footbridge. Bland went into partnership with Thomas Henry Chance, owner of the *Gloucester Journal*, in 1879 and the two papers co-located. Following a fire in 1931, the offices were rebuilt on the left of the lane, where the *Citizen* remained for the next seventy-five years. Marks & Spencer in Northgate Street took over the old site (see pp. 28–9); the rear entrance to the store can be seen in the modern picture. The *Citizen* was one of the first local papers to be computerised and the printing moved out to Staverton Technology Park in 1988. In 2007 the offices were moved to Cheltenham to co-locate with the *Cheltenham Echo*, breaking its long association with Gloucester. The old Citizen offices are now home to a ladies' gym and just a small regional office remains in the Oxebode.

*(Gloucestershire Archives / Darrel Kirby)*

# CALIFORNIA CROSSING

THESE PICTURES ARE taken from near the park on what is now Trier Way, formerly Parkend Road. The older picture, probably taken in the 1960s, harks back to the days when Gloucester had two railway stations: the Great Western, which stood where the current railway station is, and the Midland Railway, which stood roughly where Asda is today. The two were linked by a wooden footbridge 190 yards long – the longest of its kind in Britain.

The Bristol & Birmingham Railway line ran from the Midland Railway station, crossed Barton Street and then ran alongside the aptly named Midland Road. These pictures show the level crossing between Parkend Road and Midland Road. It was known as California Crossing because, for reasons probably lost in the mists of time, the area was known as California. The Midland station closed in 1975, but the course of the line can still be seen as a grassy embankment alongside Midland Road and can in fact still be traced on maps through to Tuffley. The signal-box, which can just be seen on the far left of the older picture, is now preserved at the Gloucestershire Warwickshire Railway at Toddington. The Rolls-Royce in the modern picture is probably not a standard feature.

*(Gloucestershire Archives /*
*Ken Jacques)*

# SHERBORNE STREET

NOT MUCH REMAINS from this original picture of Sherborne Street – indeed I can't be completely sure that the later picture is taken from exactly the same place. Sherborne Street was in the heart of that part of Kingsholm unofficially known as Clapham. The concept of Clapham originated in the early 1820s; the brainchild of George Worrall Counsel, it was built to provide housing for workers flocking to Gloucester as the coming of the railways and canal plunged it into the industrial revolution. Building commenced in 1822, and a decade later a total of ten streets with tiny, identical, back-to-back two-up, two-down terraced houses with lean-to sculleries and backyard privies was completed.

There were four coal yards, slaughter houses, a leather works, a foundry and Johnny's pickles factory as well as no fewer than ten pubs in the small area of Clapham. Judging by the bunting, the older picture here was taken around the time of Queen Elizabeth II's coronation in 1953. Sadly, this was towards the end of Clapham's days. As the industrial revolution waned, poverty and unemployment became rife and conditions became squalid. Between 1956 and 1957 the bulldozers moved in and Clapham was demolished.

*(Reflections of Clapham / Ken Jacques)*

# EASTGATE MARKET

THE SOUTH SIDE of Eastgate Street has almost entirely been rebuilt. The first thing that catches the eye in the older picture is the impressive market portico in the centre. Here it is in its original position, where it was built to form the entrance to the Eastgate Market when it was rebuilt in 1856. In 1973 this area was redeveloped and a huge store, formerly housing Woolworths, was built on the site and the market portico was moved to the east to form the entrance to the shiny new Eastgate Shopping Centre.

At the time the modern picture was taken, in 2011, the store has lain empty since the collapse of Woolworths in 2009 and plans have been announced for Marks & Spencer to move in. Everything to the left of the market portico was demolished to make way for the new shopping centre, including the Market House Inn, built on the site of the less-grand Eastgate Vaults, which closed in 1957. To the right, the building which housed Hardys is about all that's still recognisable. Next door to that was Currys, a significantly larger store than the one in the old picture, but that too became empty in 2011.

*(Author's Collection / Darrel Kirby)*

# THE CORN EXCHANGE

THESE PICTURES ARE taken looking down Southgate Street from the Cross, and many of the buildings on the right-hand side remain the same. One glaring change, however, is the disappearance of the Corn Exchange, shown in the foreground of the old picture. Gloucester was a market town from medieval times and in the mid-1780s two shiny new markets were built to stop them from cluttering up the streets: one in Eastgate Street (see pp. 22–3) and one in Southgate Street.

The Southgate market was rebuilt in 1856 and opened in 1857 as a corn exchange. Designed by Medland and Maberly, it had a tall Corinthian portico forming a semicircular bay and surmounted by a statue of Ceres. In 1893, shortly after this picture was taken, the front was rebuilt flush with the street frontage and part of the building became the post office. This impressive building was demolished in 1938. One thing that does remain from the original picture is the clock on the left, above Bakers the jewellers. This is part of an elaborate striking clock with figures representing England, Ireland, Scotland and Wales together with Old Father Time.

*(Gloucestershire Archives / Darrel Kirby)*

# BON MARCHÉ/
# DEBENHAMS

THIS WONDERFUL OLD PHOTOGRAPH is dated 1904 and shows the early days of the Bon Marché. The Bon Marché was started in 1889 as a drapery business by John Rowe Pope and in the picture it occupies the tall building and the one to its right. Business boomed and in 1909 the store was extended to the left. The ornate building in the foreground of the modern picture is this extension with a second, identical extension, built in 1914, next to it.

These dates are engraved at the top of the façades, which were just freshly repainted as part of the store refurbishment in September 2011. Unfortunately, these extensions necessitated the demolition of the Dolphin Vaults, seen in the small building in the foreground of the old picture. This pub had been there since at least 1722. The original Bon Marché store was demolished in 1931 and the huge monolithic new building was put up in its place, forming part of the Oxebode redevelopment. The store changed its name to Debenhams in the 1970s, although many of Gloucester's older residents never really got the hang of it and continued to call it the 'Bon Marsh' for many years.

*(Author's Collection / Darrel Kirby)*

# MARKS & SPENCER

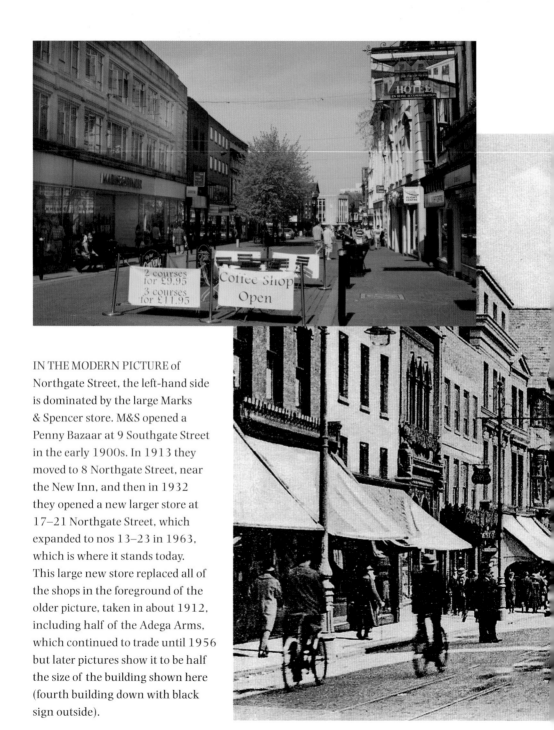

IN THE MODERN PICTURE of
Northgate Street, the left-hand side
is dominated by the large Marks
& Spencer store. M&S opened a
Penny Bazaar at 9 Southgate Street
in the early 1900s. In 1913 they
moved to 8 Northgate Street, near
the New Inn, and then in 1932
they opened a new larger store at
17–21 Northgate Street, which
expanded to nos 13–23 in 1963,
which is where it stands today.
This large new store replaced all of
the shops in the foreground of the
older picture, taken in about 1912,
including half of the Adega Arms,
which continued to trade until 1956
but later pictures show it to be half
the size of the building shown here
(fourth building down with black
sign outside).

At the time of writing it is anticipated that M&S will move into the old Woolworths building in Eastgate Street, which has been empty since Woolworths ceased trading in January 2009. The building with the prominent gable slightly further down in the older picture was Boots the Chemist, which occupied a mock-Tudor building built shortly after the First World War. Boots moved to a new store in Eastgate Street in 1980 and this store was demolished. A much less impressive building currently housing Peacocks is now on the site.

*(Author's Collection / Darrel Kirby)*

# TOLSEY

THE OLD PICTURE here, taken in about 1892, shows the Tolsey sitting on the corner of Southgate and Westgate streets. This was the main seat of government in the city. A building on this site was probably used for the purpose by 1455, but it was not known as the Tolsey until 1507. In 1751 the Tolsey was rebuilt as the impressive two-storey classical building seen here, with a carving of the city arms and insignia on the pediment facing Westgate Street. Unfortunately it became increasingly unsuitable for managing city administration and by 1889 the city officers had moved out to the nearby Corn Exchange in Southgate Street (see pp. 24–5), moving into the new Guildhall when it opened in 1892. The Tolsey was sold by the corporation and in 1893 it was demolished to make way for the Wilts and Dorset Banking Co., which opened in 1895. This is the building that stands there today and, as the modern photo shows, it is quite an imposing building. Sadly, it has been an eyesore over recent years. It was home to Hawkshead for some time, but remained empty after they vacated in 2007. In 2010 Gift's Direct [*sic*] moved in, but surely such a prime location deserves a major retailer?

*(Gloucestershire Archives / Darrel Kirby)*

# DUKE OF NORFOLK'S HOUSE

THE OLD PICTURE here can easily be dated to 1947: the year of the great floods. The floods were undoubtedly a disaster for the buildings of Lower Westgate Street, condemning them to demolition. But it is only because of the *Citizen*'s record of these floods that we have any photographic record at all of many of the old properties in Westgate Street. On the far left are two pubs: the Old Dial and the White Swan, separated by Swan Lane.

The ornate building next door to the White Swan is Eagle House, which was built in 1724. In 1788 a spring said to have medicinal properties was discovered behind it; at this time it was owned by the 11th Duke of Norfolk, so became more commonly known as the Duke of Norfolk's House. The Duke of Norfolk's House was Grade II listed, and the city corporation tried hard to find a buyer for it so it could be incorporated into the Westgate development. Unfortunately it was in a poor state of repair so there were no takers and it was finally demolished in 1971. The modern flats built in its place are known as the Dukeries.

*(Gloucestershire Media / Darrel Kirby)*

# ROBERT RAIKES'S HOUSE

THIS MARVELLOUS TIMBER-FRAMED building in Southgate Street has changed little over the years. It was built in 1560 as a merchant's house and has been described as a good example of West Country decorative timber-framing. For many years it was used as a grocery and wine and spirit store, as shown in the older picture. In more recent times, the larger part of the building became the Dirty Duck Restaurant in 1973 and a few years later it became a pub called The Golden Cross. The building had seen better days when brewers Samuel Smiths took it over and spent two years and a reported £4.5 million to renovate it, opening it in November 2008 as Robert Raikes's House. It is so called because Robert Raikes, founder of the Sunday School movement and editor of the *Gloucester Journal*, published the paper here from 1758 and lived here with his family from 1772. The restoration has been very well done; it has stripped the building back to its original state, but reflecting the extensions and alterations of the eighteenth and nineteenth centuries. Inside there are seven separate rooms, each individually furnished and the original large walled courtyard has also been resurrected behind the pub.

*(Author's Collection / Darrel Kirby)*

35

# BEARLAND
# FIRE STATION

THE MAIN BUILDING in this picture, on the corner of
Longsmith Street and Barbican Road, next door to Bearland
House, was once Gloucester's fire station. The original picture
was taken shortly after it opened on 17 July 1913 and it hasn't
changed a great deal since. The city got its first mechanical
fire engine in 1648 and from 1838 the police force trained
as fire-fighters, but most fire-fighting in the late nineteenth
century was done by insurance companies. The trouble with
this arrangement was that if you didn't happen to be insured
by the company that turned up, they just went away again. In
1912 the insurance companies hung up their hosepipes and
donated their equipment to the corporation, who set up a city
fire brigade. The building shown here remained in use as the
city's fire station until 1956, when it moved out to Eastern
Avenue.

It was adapted as a transport museum in 1977 but has now been converted to apartments, although the training tower remains. The building to the right of the original picture was the county magistrates' courts until the early 1960s when they were demolished to make way for the police station.

*(Gloucestershire Archives / Darrel Kirby)*

# KING'S SQUARE

KING'S SQUARE IS CURRENTLY perhaps the most maligned and unloved part of Gloucester, but as the older photograph here shows it was not always so. This photograph must have been taken shortly after King's Square was opened in 1974. Work on the square actually started in the 1920s as part of the Oxebode redevelopment, with shops starting to appear in the 1940s. Hitler put the mockers on further development with the outbreak of the Second World War, leaving the area as a rather unlovely bus station and car park. Development started again in 1969, resulting in the square shown in the picture.

The ambitious, modern design was so impressive that it won the Civic Trust award in 1972. Unfortunately neither the design nor the structure aged well and by the 1980s it was falling into decline. In 2006, the area was levelled as an interim solution prior to redevelopment. At the time of writing in 2011, plans are finally afoot to do something about it as part of the 'King's Quarter' development, but I can't help wondering whether in the future people will castigate us for destroying such a wonderful example of 1970s architecture in the same way that we bemoan the destruction of medieval and Victorian buildings today.

*(Author's Collection / Darrel Kirby)*

# ST OSWALD'S PRIORY

THESE TWO PICTURES show the remains of St Oswald's Priory. Since the older picture was
taken, probably at the end of the nineteenth century, little has changed, although some slight
remodelling can be seen and it underwent cleaning and renovation in about 2007. St Oswald's
Priory is probably the oldest upstanding building in the city, dating from around AD 890 when
the minster was founded by Aethelflaed, daughter of Alfred the Great and wife of Aethelred,
lord of the Mercians. The original minster was probably partly built with stone quarried
from one of the great Roman public buildings that were still littering up the place. In AD 909
Aethelflaed and her brother Edward, King of Wessex, led a daring raid into Danish territory in
Lincolnshire, snatching the bones of St Oswald, seventh-century king and saint, which were
laid to rest in the new minster. It is possible that Aethelflaed herself was buried here.

By the time of its
dissolution in 1536, the
church of St Oswald's was
ruinous. What was left was
adapted into the parish
church of St Catherine
in 1548. It was badly
damaged during the Siege
of Gloucester in 1643 and
was demolished in 1653.
*(Author's Collection /
Darrel Kirby)*

# GREYFRIARS

THIS IS A fascinating picture taken by a lady called Gwladys Davies, probably in the early 1960s. It shows the old Greyfriars ruins incorporated into business premises including, as you can see, the Liberal Party Headquarters (who may or may not turn up by motorcycle and side car). Greyfriars was the home of the Franciscan friars, who founded their house in Gloucester in 1231. With remarkably bad timing the friary was rebuilt in 1518, just twenty years before Henry VIII dissolved the monasteries. It was almost immediately converted into a brewery, making use of the fresh water supply that the monks had piped in from Robinswood Hill.

The building suffered badly during the Siege of Gloucester in 1643 and subsequently the ruins were filled in as shown in the older picture here. These additions were removed in the 1960s – a rare example of history being preserved in that era – revealing the ruins as they appear today, squeezed in between the back of the Eastgate Shopping Centre and the old Gloscat building. At the time of writing in 2011, the Greyfriars development is commencing, not without some controversy, to redevelop the old Gloscat building and hopefully display the ruins in a more sympathetic environment.

*(Gloucestershire Archives / Darrel Kirby)*

# ST BARTHOLOMEW'S ALMSHOUSE

THE BOTTOM OF WESTGATE STREET is known as 'the Island'. Today this is appropriate as it is a large roundabout surrounded by the busy roads leading to and from Westgate Bridge. Originally, however, it was an island in the more traditional sense, sitting between two branches of the Severn, the now vanished Old Severn and the still existing East Channel.

The older of these pictures looking up Westgate Street from the Island was taken before the ring road was built in 1961, demolishing all of the buildings apart from the one in the foreground: St Bartholomew's Almshouse.

St Bartholomew's originated as a house for workers building Westgate Bridge in the twelfth century. It was subsequently used as a hospital and by the sixteenth century it was the largest and wealthiest of the three ancient hospitals in Gloucester (the other two being St Mary Magdalene's and St Margaret's, both in London Road). By 1789 the building was pulled down and replaced by the current Gothic-style building, designed by local architect William Price. It was sold in 1971 and restored and reopened in 1985 as the Westgate Galleria shopping centre. It underwent another £1 million facelift in 2006 to become Westgate Business Centre.

*(Gloucestershire Archives / Darrel Kirby)*

# ST MARY DE CRYPT

Gloucester. St. Mary de Crypt Church.

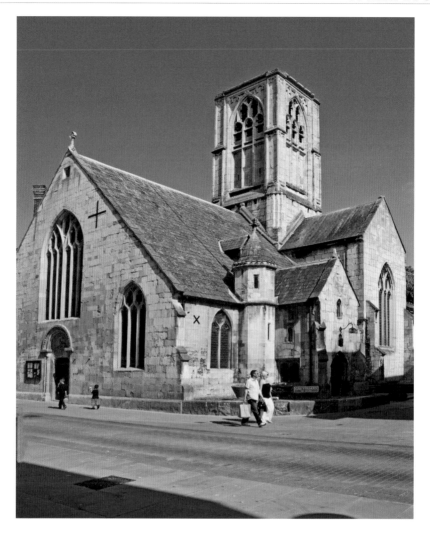

ST MARY DE CRYPT is on the east side of Southgate Street. A church was first recorded on this site in the 1140s, but it has Roman foundations. In 1241 the church was granted to Llanthony Priory. It was considerably rebuilt in the fifteenth century by Henry Dene, prior of Llanthony Secunda and later Archbishop of Canterbury. By the early sixteenth century the church looked pretty much as it does in the old photograph here, taken in 1891. There is a sundial set into the buttress on the south-east corner of the chancel which allegedly marks the point of impact of a Royalist cannonball during the Civil War of 1643. George Whitefield, the famous Methodist preacher, preached his first sermon in the church shortly after being ordained a deacon in 1736 and the pulpit he used is still in the nave today. Robert Raikes, founder of the Sunday School movement, was both baptised and buried in the church. Extensive restoration to the fabric of the church was undertaken in the 1840s, but the main change between the two photographs shown here is due to the removal of the impressively ornate battlements and pinnacles in 1908 as they were unsafe.

*(Author's Collection / Darrel Kirby)*

# ST MICHAEL'S CHURCH

THIS SCENE OF the south side of Eastgate Street near the Cross has changed completely; the main change being the demolition of most of St Michael's Church. Built on the site of a Saxon church, it was in existence in the twelfth century. It extended about 80ft down Eastgate Street, enclosing a burial ground on the south side. The church was rebuilt between 1455 and 1472, and the tower that still exists today dates from about 1465. The north wall of the church encroached into the street, so the whole main body of the church apart from the tower was demolished in 1849 and a new, larger church incorporating the old tower was erected slightly further to the south in 1851.

In 1940 St Michael's parish combined with St Mary de Crypt and the church closed. It was demolished in 1956 leaving only the tower, which is Grade II listed and is now used by the Civic Trust who extensively renovated it in 2009. The other prominent building in the older photograph is the Greyhound Hotel. Recorded from 1544, the hotel closed in the 1920s and Botherways, whose shop can be seen next door, opened a café on the site, later becoming the fondly remembered Cadena Café.

*(Author's Collection / Darrel Kirby)*

# ST NICHOLAS' CHURCH

THESE PICTURES SHOW St Nicholas' Church, whose tall spire dominates Lower Westgate Street. The church originates from about 1190 and parts of the original Norman building can still be seen, its antiquity suggested by the fact that the church floor is significantly below street level.

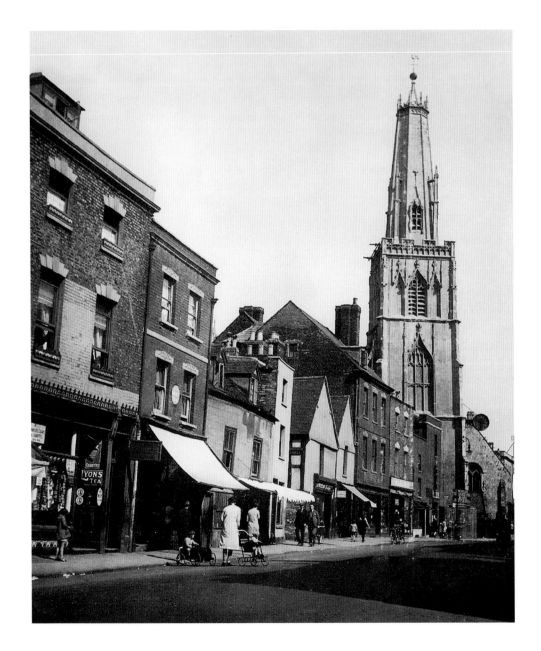

The church's spire was once even more imposing, measuring about 200ft tall. Unfortunately It took a direct hit in the Civil War and was never fully stable after that, so in 1783 it was shortened. It is still slightly crooked. In 1952 the parish of St Nicholas was united with the parish of St Mary de Lode and in 1971 the church was declared redundant. The row of buildings in the foreground of the older picture are now all gone. They were demolished as part of the Westgate Comprehensive Redevelopment, which started after the Second World War, and replaced with the flats that you see today. These are set significantly further back from the road and in 1961 a controversial modern sculpture entitled The Family was erected in the square in front of them. After being the target of vandals for many years this was finally taken down in 1980 and broken up.

*(Author's Collection / Darrel Kirby)*

# PARK STREET
# MISSION ROOMS

THE OLDER PICTURE here shows the Park Street Mission Rooms in the early 1900s. As the name suggests, it is located in Park Street, which originally ran parallel to Hare Lane but today both are pretty much merged into a large car park. The site was originally occupied by two cottages in what was then a rural and fairly isolated suburb. In those days of religious intolerance and persecution such isolation had its benefits and the cottages were purchased in 1678 to be used by Quakers (then called Children of the Light) as a meeting house. The gardens at the rear became their burial ground. The Quakers moved to the present Friends Meeting House which opened in Greyfriars in 1834, and in 1867 the Park Street mission was established in their former meeting house. The original building was replaced by the building shown in the modern picture in 1903. The mission obviously had less cause for discretion as the new building has 'PARK STREET MISSION ROOM' boldly etched in the lintel at the top of the building and is still very clear today should anyone queueing to get out of the car park choose to look up slightly.

*(Gloucestershire Archives / Darrel Kirby)*

# NORTHGATE
# METHODIST CHURCH

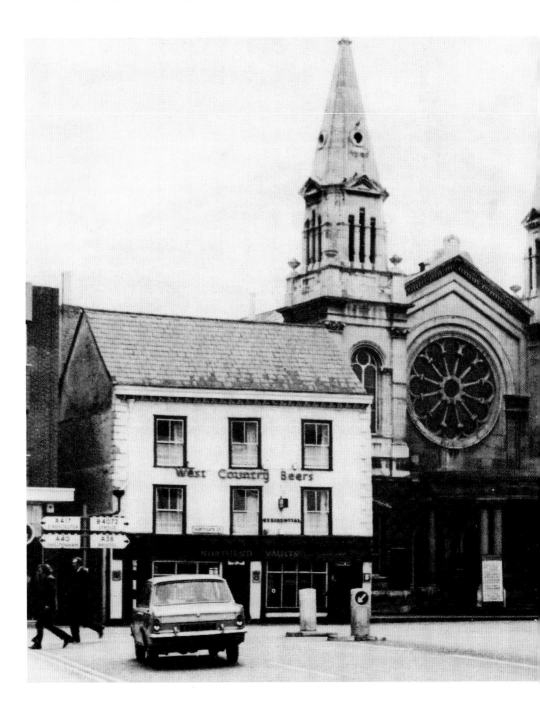

THIS IS THE JUNCTION of Worcester Street and Northgate Street. The dominant building in the older photograph, probably taken in the 1960s, is the Northgate Methodist Church – a magnificent building with an imposing portico, twin towers and large rose window. Built in the nineteenth century it replaced a small chapel on the site, built in 1787, where Wesley preached on several occasions. The Methodist church joined with St John's further up Northgate Street in 1972 and it was pulled down in the late 1970s, so now when you enter the city from the north you are instead met with the less than impressive, huge, bland-to-the-point-of-ugly store currently occupied by Wilkinson's. This was formerly Tesco until the 1980s when it moved to the first big out-of-town hypermarket in Quedgeley. By contrast, the smaller building to the left has miraculously survived intact. It dates back to the late sixteenth or early seventeenth century, when it was a merchant's house. It was refronted in the eighteenth century, but behind that is the original timber-framed building. It was a pub by 1869; originally called the Northend Vaults it is now known simply as the Vaults.

*(Reg Woolford / Ken Jacques)*

# CRYPT SCHOOL ROOM

THE OLD CRYPT School Room is situated next to St Mary de Crypt Church (see pp. 46–7). The frontage shown in these pictures is faced with stone and incorporates an archway over St Mary's Lane or Marylone. The rear elevation of the schoolroom, overlooking the churchyard, is one of the earliest examples of Tudor brickwork to be found in the region. The Crypt Schoolroom was constructed in 1539 to provide free education in competition with the fee-paying school provided by the Prior of Llanthony Priory.

Initiated by John Cooke, a wealthy mercer and four times mayor of the city, it was realised after his death by his widow Joan. The Crypt School continued on this site until 1861 and both George Whitefield and Robert Raikes are counted as old boys. It then moved to Barton Street, and in 1889 it moved again to Friars Orchard on Brunswick Road, the site occupied until recently by the Gloscat (see pp. 62–3). In 1943 it moved for a final time to a new building at Podsmead. Meanwhile, the original schoolroom was restored and reopened in 1880 as St Mary de Crypt Sunday School in memory of Robert Raikes. It is currently in use as the church hall.

*(Author's Collection / Darrel Kirby)*

# SUNDAY SCHOOL

THESE PHOTOGRAPHS SHOW the junction of St Catherine Street and Park Street, known as St Catherine's Knapp. The impressive building to the left of the older picture, probably taken in the 1890s, was Robert Raikes's first Sunday School for girls. Apparently Raikes was in St Catherine Street when he noticed ragged children playing in the street and decided they needed somewhere to go. He opened the first Sunday School in St Catherine Street in 1780, but that was just for boys; the girls' version followed a couple of years later.

Unfortunately the building was demolished in the 1950s and the area was left as rubble-strewn wasteground for many years before the modern apartments were built. The other building does still survive: the Coach & Horses Inn. Although today it is in a bit of a back street, originally it was a prime location at the end of Hare Lane, the main route in and out of the city to the north until Worcester Street was built in the 1820s. The building dates back to the early sixteenth century and it was an inn by the eighteenth century. The pub's name and location both suggest that it would have been a coaching inn.

*(Author's Collection / Darrel Kirby)*

# SCHOOL OF SCIENCE & ART

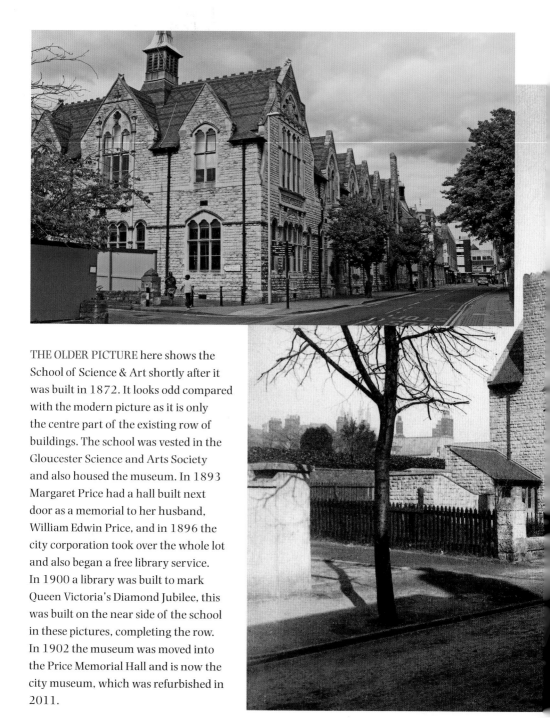

THE OLDER PICTURE here shows the School of Science & Art shortly after it was built in 1872. It looks odd compared with the modern picture as it is only the centre part of the existing row of buildings. The school was vested in the Gloucester Science and Arts Society and also housed the museum. In 1893 Margaret Price had a hall built next door as a memorial to her husband, William Edwin Price, and in 1896 the city corporation took over the whole lot and also began a free library service. In 1900 a library was built to mark Queen Victoria's Diamond Jubilee, this was built on the near side of the school in these pictures, completing the row. In 1902 the museum was moved into the Price Memorial Hall and is now the city museum, which was refurbished in 2011.

In 1941 the science school moved to the new Technical College built on Friars Orchard further up Brunswick Road (see pp. 62–3); the art school stayed where it was and was renamed the College of Art in 1952. It moved to the opposite side of Brunswick Road in 1968, becoming the Gloucestershire College of Art and Design. At this time presumably the library was enlarged into the vacated building.

*(Gloucestershire Archives / Darrel Kirby)*

# TECHNICAL COLLEGE

THE GLOUCESTERSHIRE COLLEGE of Art and Technology, known more pithily as Gloscat, was located at two sites on Brunswick Road. These pictures show the main site; the 'media site' was on the other side of the road opposite the library. Originally just called the Technical College, it was built on land known as Friars Orchard. These were once the grounds of Greyfriars, but were acquired by the Crypt School in 1888. The building shown here was built between 1938 and 1941 in the art deco style. The older photograph shows it in the 1960s. The newer photograph, taken in early 2011, shows it in a sad state of decay as in 2007 Gloscat moved to a modern new building on the docks.

The Gloscat building is in the City Centre Conservation Area and is of archaeological interest because the Roman city wall passes in front of the site. It is now part of the Gloucester Heritage Urban Regeneration Company's Greyfriars redevelopment and as I write the site is boarded up and work has begun to create a new development of houses, restaurants and retail buildings. Despite local opposition, this building has been condemned to demolition.

*(Gloucestershire Archives / Darrel Kirby)*

# DOCKS MAIN BASIN

THE GLOUCESTER DOCKS are the terminus of the Gloucester and Sharpness Canal, which opened for business in 1827. These pictures are looking across the main basin, which opened before the canal, in 1812. Much remains the same: the warehouse in the centre distance is the North Warehouse; built between 1826 and 1827 it is the oldest warehouse in the docks. It was saved from demolition in 1980 and is currently used as administrative offices for Gloucester City Council.

The warehouses on the east side of the basin are the Herbert, Kimberley and (not visible in the older picture) Philpotts warehouses. Built in 1846 for the corn trade these were the first warehouses to be renovated in 1985 and they house offices, except Kimberley Warehouse which also houses a pub, Foster's on the Docks. The main difference between the two pictures, apart from the change from commercial to pleasure craft, is the warehouses on the left. The older picture shows a range of eight warehouses built by Birmingham corn merchants Joseph and Charles Sturge between 1829 and 1831. These were demolished in 1966 and modern new apartments, appropriately called the West Quay, were built on the site in 2005.

*(Author's Collection / Ken Jacques)*

# LLANTHONY BRIDGE

THESE PICTURES ARE taken from Bakers Quay looking north towards Llanthony Bridge and the main basin of Gloucester Docks. The old picture was taken in about 1900 and shows the original Llanthony Bridge, a swing bridge installed in 1862. This was replaced by a lifting bridge in the 1970s, as shown in the modern picture. Beware if you are driving in the area today as the bridge is now closed to traffic and you could face a hefty fine for crossing it.

The other main difference between the two pictures is the disappearance of the large warehouse on the far left. This was the Great Western Warehouse; built in 1863 it was destroyed by fire in 1945 while being used by a firm producing breakfast cereal. Most of the warehouse was demolished, but the ground floor was retained and given a new roof. The small warehouse next to it was a large wooden shed which has now been replaced by a brick building somewhat unimaginatively called No. 4 Warehouse. Next to that is the Alexandra Warehouse; built in 1870 for storing corn and later sugar, it remains largely unchanged on the outside, but inside it is now put to general business use.

*(Gloucestershire Archives /*
*Ken Jacques)*

# HIGH ORCHARD STREET

THESE PICTURES LOOK down High Orchard Street from Llanthony Road. In medieval times this area was the high orchard of Llanthony Priory, but it was separated when the canal was cut through it. Baker's Quay was built on this part of the canal and a variety of industries sprang up around it including, in the 1890s, a huge furniture factory, Matthew's Cabinet Works, which ran the length of High Orchard Street on the east side.

The Atlas Iron Works was built to the south-east of High Orchard Street, where Fielding & Platt was founded in 1866. All of this industry was served by sidings from the Midland Railway's High Orchard goods yard just to the south. Matthew's closed in 1935 and the premises were put to a variety of other uses. Fielding & Platt, one of Gloucester's last heavy engineering companies, moved to Leeds in 2000. The whole area had long-since fallen into a sorry state of dereliction by the time this older picture was taken in December 2006. Things have changed markedly now, however, as the whole area has been transformed into the £400 million Gloucester Quays Designer Outlet, which opened in May 2009.

*(Both photographs Ken Jacques)*

# GLOUCESTER RAILWAY CARRIAGE AND WAGON COMPANY

THE OLDER PICTURE here was taken in 1910 and shows the offices of Gloucester Railway Carriage and Wagon Company (GRCW) in Bristol Road, opposite the junction to Stroud Road, draped in memory of the late King Edward VII. The company covered a large area between Southgate Street and the canal, but there is little evidence left of it today.

The company, originally much more pithily named the Gloucester Wagon Co. Ltd, started in 1860 to make, repair and hire railway trucks. It built up foreign trade, eventually becoming world famous. Having diversified to include railway carriages, in 1887 it changed its name to Gloucester Railway Carriage & Wagon Co. Ltd. By the end of the nineteenth century it was the largest employer in Gloucester with a workforce of over 1,100 people. The original offices were pulled down in 1904 to make way for this much grander building. In 1961 the GRCW was acquired by Wingets Ltd and then in 1986 they were taken over by Babcock Industrial & Electrical Products Ltd. In 1989 the redundant offices along with the rest of the wagon works buildings were demolished to make way for the Peel Centre. The former carriage erecting shop still exists as a karting centre.

*(Gloucestershire Archives / Ken Jacques)*

# GRCW SHOWROOM

THE GLOUCESTER RAILWAY CARRIAGE AND WAGON COMPANY (GRCW) was located in Bristol Road (see previous page) but they built two showrooms to show off their wares nearer to the city centre. The one shown here was the first of these, built in 1894 in what was then George Street, near to the railway station. Modern road changes mean that it is now on the corner of London Road and Bruton Way.

The showroom was used to display horse-drawn carriages, and interestingly the sign above the door bears the name Gloucester Carriage and Wheel Works, who GRCW took over the previous year. It was sold to the Post Office in 1904 and later became a retail outlet for Dunelm Mill fabric shop. They moved out and the building lay empty for a number of years, becoming an eyesore, before being taken over by Gloucester-based architects Roberts Limbrick Limited, who restored it beautifully in 2011. The second showroom was built in 1898 on the opposite side of George Street near the cattle market. It was converted to a corn exchange in 1923, then in the late 1930s became a popular dance hall called Prince's Hall. The Bruton Way multi-storey car park is now on the site.

*(Gloucestershire Archives / Darrel Kirby)*

# MORELANDS' MATCH FACTORY

THE OLDER PICTURE here was taken in 1976 and shows a surprisingly cheery-looking bunch of workers staging a demonstration outside the Morelands' Match Factory as it was threatened with closure. The dancing and demonstrations were ultimately unsuccessful, however, and the factory closed with the loss of 280 jobs. The decision to close must have come as a shock as until that point the factory appeared to be doing well.

Morelands was started in 1867 by Samuel John Moreland, a timber merchant from Stroud. He opened a small factory in Bristol Road close to the canal the following year. The current factory was built in the 1890s and enlarged in 1911, when the first continuous, automated match-making machinery was installed, increasing production to 360,000 boxes of matches per week. At its peak, Morelands produced forty brands and 50 million matches per day. Their most famous brand, England's Glory, was adopted in 1891 and continued after the company was acquired by Bryant & May in 1913. Morelands factory was reopened as a trading estate in 1978. Little has changed externally, except some of the smaller buildings have been removed to widen the entrance. The England's Glory sign, erected in 1954, is still in place.

*(Gloucestershire Media / Darrel Kirby)*

# THE SPA

THESE TWO PHOTOGRAPHS of Gloucester Spa look very similar except for one very important difference: in the modern picture the spa building has gone! The area was known as the Rigney Style grounds and a spring was discovered here in 1814. The waters were proclaimed as containing more health-giving properties than any so far discovered in the country.

The landowner, Sir James Jelf, formed a Spa Company and the pump room opened to subscribers in 1815. The southern end of Brunswick Road, where these photographs were taken from, was widened, providing an imposing approach to the pump room. Elegant, fashionable houses were built near the spa beginning in 1816 in what was then called Norfolk Street, but which became Spa Road. However, the spa in Cheltenham was already popular and Gloucester's was less fashionable. Even though its waters were said to have better medicinal properties, by the late 1820s Gloucester Spa was in decline and in 1861 its grounds were acquired by the city corporation and included into Gloucester Park. The springs were closed in 1894 and became contaminated in 1926. After years of neglect by the city authorities the pump room was demolished in 1960.

*(Gloucestershire Archives / Darrel Kirby)*

# GLOUCESTER PARK

GLOUCESTER PARK's magnificent fountain was removed from the Eastgate Market in the 1920s. It has long since stopped acting as a fountain and is now planted up as a flower bed. The park itself was opened by the city corporation in 1862 and includes the former spa grounds (see previous page). After a long period of neglect, the park has been transformed in recent years and is once again a pleasant recreational site for the city, as the Victorians intended. As well as the fountain it contains a statue of Robert Raikes, founder of the Sunday School movement; a war memorial; and a bandstand: a modern structure erected in 2010 which controversially replaced the previous brick and bath stone bandstand built in 1933.

It was mid-December before the tree had shed enough leaves to reveal a glimpse of the church in the background for our modern photograph. This is the Whitefield Memorial Church on Park Road. Built to mark the centenary of the death of the famous evangelical preacher George Whitefield, who was born in Gloucester in 1714, it was founded in 1872. Its magnificent spire was taken down in the 1970s.

*(Author's Collection / Ken Jacques)*

# THE THEATRE ROYAL

THESE PICTURES OF Westgate Street show that many of the buildings remain largely unchanged. One exception is the building on the far left in the original photograph, taken by Sidney Pitcher in the 1890s. This was a theatre, which opened in 1791 and was called the Theatre Royal from the late 1830s. In 1903 it was acquired by Poole's, who renamed it the Palace of Varieties, then later the Palace Theatre. In 1911 it became a cinema and was closed by 1922 when Poole's acquired the Hippodrome in Eastgate Street.

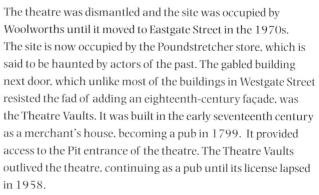

The theatre was dismantled and the site was occupied by Woolworths until it moved to Eastgate Street in the 1970s. The site is now occupied by the Poundstretcher store, which is said to be haunted by actors of the past. The gabled building next door, which unlike most of the buildings in Westgate Street resisted the fad of adding an eighteenth-century façade, was the Theatre Vaults. It was built in the early seventeenth century as a merchant's house, becoming a pub in 1799. It provided access to the Pit entrance of the theatre. The Theatre Vaults outlived the theatre, continuing as a pub until its license lapsed in 1958.

*(Gloucestershire Archives / Darrel Kirby)*

# THE PICTUREDROME

THE OLD PICTURE here shows the corner of Barton Street and Blenheim Road. This was previously a pleasure ground called the Blenheim Gardens, which opened in 1812 and later became known as the Vauxhall Gardens. The gardens were built on from 1863 when more housing was required for workers attracted by the city's burgeoning industry. A cinema called Palmers Picturedrome was built on the corner in 1923.

Initially owned by the Gloucester Cinema Company, by 1943 it had been acquired by the ABC chain, who renamed it the Ritz. Unfortunately, the cinema was fairly far down the pecking order when it came to showing new releases, so it wasn't very popular and it closed in 1962. It almost immediately reopened as the Alpha Bingo Club, which was taken over by Mecca in 1966. Mecca left in 1984 and it was bought by the Gloucester Operatic & Dramatic Society to replace their small Olympus Theatre in Kings Barton Street. They renamed it the New Olympus Theatre and in 1991 it was given a make-over by the BBC1 series *Challenge Anneka*. It was bought by two local businessmen in about 2009 and the name reverted to the Picturedrome. It is still in use as a theatre.

*(Gloucestershire Archives / Ken Jacques)*

# THE NEW INN

THESE PICTURES SHOW the courtyard of the magnificent New Inn in Northgate Street. Built by St Peter's Abbey (now the cathedral) between 1430 and 1450, it was one of the Great Inns of the Abbey. It has two tiers of galleries which originally provided accommodation for up to 200 people: 40 sleeping rooms, some in the form of dormitories. At this time it was said to be the largest hostelry in the country.

It is from these galleries that in 1553 the news of Lady Jane Grey's coronation was broadcast: a proclamation that was only made publicly in two other places in England. To commemorate the occasion the inn now has a Lady Jane Grey suite. There is speculation that Shakespeare may have played at the New Inn in the sixteenth century and by 1649 it also housed the city's first tennis court. In the eighteenth century the inn became an important venue on the London to Gloucester stage coach route. The New Inn was bought by Berni Inns in 1954 and during their ownership the inn boasted thirteen separate bars. Since the 1980s it has had a series of owners and is now owned by the Chapman Group.

*(Author's Collection / Ken Jacques)*

# THE FLEECE HOTEL

THESE PICTURES LOOK down Westgate Street away from the Cross, with St Nicholas' Church in the centre. In the foreground on the left is the Fleece Hotel, which stands out much more in the modern picture than the older one. The Fleece Hotel, like the New Inn (see previous page), was one of Gloucester's Great Inns of the Abbey. The original part of the inn, which can't be seen as it sits behind the buildings fronting the street, dates back to the twelfth century and sits upon an extensive undercroft, which until quite recently was also a bar known as the Monks Retreat.

The old inn was rebuilt in 1497 and the associated buildings visible from the street were added at that time. The current appearance of the inn is an early twentieth-century con: the timber frame and brick buildings were rendered and boards were applied to give the impression of a half-timbered building. The Fleece closed in October 2002 and fell into a poor state of repair. In 2011 the council bought it from the defunct South West Regional Development Agency and work has begun to bring it back into use with completion planned for 2016.

*(Author's Collection / Darrel Kirby)*

# THE BELL HOTEL

THE IMPRESSIVE MAIN building in this picture was the Bell Hotel, probably Gloucester's most prestigious hotel. Situated in Southgate Street it extended almost to Bell Lane, now Bell Walk. Both the inn and the lane were named for the trade of bell making, for which Gloucester was renowned. An inn existed on the site from at least 1544. The evangelist preacher George Whitefield was born there in 1714: his father was landlord.

By 1744 the Bell became a coaching inn, competing with its main rival the King's Head in Westgate Street. The two inns were also rivals in politics; with the Bell providing the headquarters for the Tories and the King's Head for the Whigs. The inn was sold to the Gloucester Bell Hotel Co. Ltd in 1864 and was rebuilt. From about 1912 the upper floors of the magnificent Jacobean building in the foreground of the picture were leased to the Bell as meeting and function rooms. These still survive as the Old Bell. The Bell Inn closed in 1967 and in 1973 it was demolished to make way for the construction of the Eastgate Shopping Centre shown in the recent picture – a sad indictment of changing building styles over the course of 100 years.

*(Author's Collection / Darrel Kirby)*

# THE RAM HOTEL

THE RAM HOTEL in Southgate Street was recorded in licensing records by 1680 and by 1791 it was one of the city's most important social centres. It was rebuilt in about 1840, which is probably when it became known as a hotel. It was the first commercial premises in Gloucester to have a telephone. In April 1887 the Western Counties & South Wales Telephone Company established an exchange in Berkeley Street. The *Gloucester Journal* wrote, 'During the past few days the Ram Hotel and the Exchange have been connected by a wire and the success of the telephonic system of communications has been demonstrated completely.' The older picture here, taken in 1910, shows

the Ram with the grand frontage added in 1890. It was later renamed the Ram & County Hotel, then after extensive refurbishment it reopened as the New County Hotel in 1937. The New County ceased trading in 2008 when the company who owned it went into administration. In 2009 it controversially opened briefly as Mystiques Hotel & Restaurant, a 'lifestyle hotel' with fantasy rooms and an adult-themed restaurant. This didn't last long and in November 2010 it reopened under new management, once again called the New County Hotel.

*(Gloucestershire Archives / Darrel Kirby)*

# THE IMPERIAL

NOT A GREAT deal has changed at the Imperial over the past 100 or so years – not externally anyway. Records of a building on this site go back to at least 1556 when a Mr John Wyman left it in his will to the 'Proctors and Parishioners of the Church of St John the Baptist'. It appears in licensing records in 1722 when it was called the Plough. It was bought by Mitchells & Butlers

in 1898, who rebuilt it in their typical ornamental style with elaborately moulded and coloured glazed tiles. These days it is Grade II listed. The old picture here was probably taken not long after it was rebuilt and the sign over the door shows the landlord as John Hyde, who is presumably the chap in the picture with his family. The interior rooms were all knocked into one in 1985, but externally the only differences in the modern picture are the missing signs on the top of the building and the elaborate lamp over the doorway. Standing proprietorially in the doorway in the modern picture is the current landlord, Tom, and his wife Karen, who have been at the Imperial since June 1990, accompanied by their grand-daughter Ruby.

*(Gloucestershire Archives / Ken Jacques)*

# BULL LANE

THE ONLY THING to hint that these two pictures are of the same place is the shape of the road; pretty much everything else has been demolished. Running between Westgate Street and Longsmith Street, it was originally called Gore Lane as it was home to pigsties and slaughter houses. The name changed to Bull Lane by 1708 for the pub that stood there. The older photograph shows the Bull Inn bearing the name of the landlord, Ernest Daniel Tandy, who was there in the 1880s. It is first found in licensing records in 1682, although it is probably much older. It closed in 1910 and the building was used as an antiques warehouse for a time until it was demolished in 1952 to make way for the extension to Gloucester telephone exchange. A large stone slab with a numbered grid on it, thought to have been used in a game and known as the Bull Stone, was found on the site and can be seen in the Folk Museum. On the left are buildings associated with the Fleece Hotel, which still survive, but beyond that everything was demolished to make way for the multi-storey car park built in Longsmith Street in the 1970s.

*(Gloucestershire Archives / Darrel Kirby)*

# FURTHER READING

Campion, Peter, *England's Glory: The Moreland Story*, Tempus Publishing, 2005

Cole, Robert, *Rental of all the Houses in Gloucester AD 1455*, John Bellows, 1890

Conway-Jones, Hugh, *Gloucester Docks: An Illustrated History*, Alan Sutton Publishing, 1984

Heighway, Carolyn, *Gloucester: A History and Guide*, Alan Sutton Publishing, 1985

Herbert, N.M. (ed), *A History of the County of Gloucester*, Vol. 4, The City of Gloucester, Oxford University Press, 1988

Jurica, John, *Gloucester: A Pictorial History*, Phillimore & Co., 1994

Kirby, Darrel, *The Story of Gloucester*, Sutton Publishing, 2007

——, *The Story of Gloucester's Pubs*, The History Press, 2010

Moss, Philip, *Historic Gloucester*, Nonsuch Publishing, 2005

Woolford, Reginald and Drake, Barbara, *Gloucester in Old Picture Postcards*, European Library, 1995


WEBSITES

A History of the County of Gloucester, Vol. 4, The City of Gloucester – www.british-history.ac.uk/source.aspx?pubid=281

Gloucester Civic Trust – www.gloucestercivictrust.org.uk/

Gloucester Docks and the Sharpness Canal: Past, Present and Future – www.gloucesterdocks.me.uk/index.htm

Gloucester Heritage Urban Regeneration Company – www.gloucesterurc.co.uk/

Gloucestershire Archives – www.gloucestershire.gov.uk/archives

The Gloucestershire Portal – www.visit-gloucestershire.co.uk/

Gloucestershire Pubs – www.gloucestershirecamra.org.uk/pubs/glospubs/new

Listed Buildings in Gloucester – www.britishlistedbuildings.co.uk/england/gloucestershire/gloucester

Also, check out my website for additional material from my books at www.darrelkirby.com